Assimilated Natives

Assimilated Natives

Gume Laurel III

MOUTHFEEL PRESS

Acknowledgements:

Thank you to Maria and Mouthfeel Press for believing in this collection. Sabrina, for helping me develop as a poet while our companionship deepens. Ashley, Bell, Christine, Roberta, and Crystal, for being sources of encouragement since the beginning of my publishing journey. Ire'ne, César, Erasmo, and Chibbi for your kind blurbs. Celeste, for years of guidance. Frankie, for the media to accompany this collection. Jon, for Marfa magic that revived this collection.

Assimilated Natives

Mouthfeel Press is an indie press publishing works in English and Spanish by new and established poets and writers. We publish poetry, fiction, and non-fiction.

Cover Design: Cloud Cardona
Photograph of the Border: Gume Laurel III

Contact Information:
Mouthfeelbooks.com
Info.mouthfeelbooks@gmail.com

ISBN: 978-1-957840-24-6
Library of Congress Control Number: 2024931364

Published in the United States, 2024

First Printing in English
$18

TABLE OF CONTENTS

Assimilated Natives

An Explanation

I am not a first generation American. I am third. After you tell the same story so many times, the narratives change. Texas Rangers morph from deputized, murderous racists to TV show heroes. Not speaking Spanish rebrands itself as having a proper education. Losing your cultural heritage is no longer losing anything.

It's fitting   in.

In this third retelling, I've minimized my heritage to fit into America so much that it's a sweater three sizes too small. It itches when I can't roll my Rs. I roll up my sleeves and work to stomach mispronouncing my name so people won't butcher it worse. My stomach peeks beneath the snug sweater when I reach out to family members over fifty in silence because we don't speak the same language.

This story takes place in the Río Grande Valley.

The southernmost borderlands of

America   &   Mexico

Deep South Texas   *El Norte*

We are neither   We are both

Sewn together by   a river splitting us in half

Even as *natives* to this land

many of us have no clue who we truly are

because we have *assimilated* for generations

to   belong
to   prosper
to   survive

An Introduction

My name is Gume
Yes, that is my real name
No, it's not my real name
My real name is Gumecindo

Pero, like, I have a tendency to sell myself short,
Cut syllables like corners
Make myself more palpable
Less to digest
Easier to stomach
I am a mouthful of heartburn

Pero, like, don't you dare call me spicy or
I'll call out your racism
I wouldn't totally hate you if you say I'm hot
On a good day, I consider myself an open blaze
Make Flamin' Hot Cheetos jealous
Make Flames of Mordor wish they could volcano
I've got hobbits, elves, and men coming at me, thinking
I want something to do with their one ring
But the idea of permanency gives me chills, so
Don't bother with a ring—text me instead
I'm a lover of words and minds

I never cash out fresh green in one sitting
I have a bad habit of leaving things unfinished
Because when I was eight years old. . .

Look. . .I have a hard time opening up

I am a sun refusing to rise if it's not cloudy enough
I need buffer room between my shine and you

Buzzfeed quiz label me an introvert
I call it laying low
No desire to be seen shining too brightly
No brown-blooded boy needs attention in a country

That wants him to go back to where he came from
Even though he's from here

I never truly know where I'm going
Especially with my words
I speak in cursive with lots of loops and circles
Taking forever
To reach the point

I left my hometown because I thought it was too small
Now, I never leave my apartment
Perhaps I'm not a size queen after all

I want to be a king of hearts
Finding enough space within myself to call home
Ace the test of time when seasons are too bitter to wear anything
Than an oversized hoodie

I want to fit in
To find a place to call my own
As time goes by, I find these two
Aren't mutually exclusive

Maybe I'm a paper origami
A swan trying to flatten out
Or maybe I'm still a tree
Firmly rooted, growing
Giving the world a breath of fresh air

I suppose this is everything I squeeze
between the *m* and *e*

when I say,
My name is Gume

Roots

"OMG so, like, what color do you want *this* time?" asks my hair stylist.
    He fumbles with my tattered, back-to-ground-brown hair,
    a tinge of cotton candy pink holds on to my split ends.
    "Silver is *so* in right now, girl."

"Silver will be fine."

I want to be *so* in.   *Right.*   *Now.*

Get down to the roots again,
strip away my natural hue,
make me forget how I'm supposed to look
when left to grow in the wild unpruned
Tame me. Rename me.

I want to be *so* in.   *Right.*   *Now.*

My hair is a construction site—
chemical dyes bulldozing
demolishing the sight
of my birthright esthetic of deep
South Texas expectation—
standard uniform—issued at the head of the line
an imprisonment chained to
my own thoughts, a walking bull's-eye
when I wear natural dark brown hair.

"Girl, this will make you a new person," my stylists beams with good intention,
    his smile painting an easier future in a city where people
    are stopped at random on Riverside and Wickersham
    and asked for identification. People
    with natural dark brown hair.

"This silver hair will make you look like you're not even *from* the valley," he winks,
    observing and capitalizing on my displaced borders,
    ignoring the swell of guilt in the glitter of my eye.

"Good,"
		I say.

"Get down to my roots."

				Right.

					Now.

Uprooted

Fields I was grown in can't give me sure footing

                              Uprooted too early   stunted growth

I should have developed a rolling tongue

                              &
                                        sun-kissed back of the neck

But this land is   This land is

      your land   *not my land*

You sweep it away

beneath my feet

                              &

                                  my roots are torn as

                                             I

                                      am

                                                ripped

                                      daily

                                  from

my

                                              homeland

A Poem Written in the Rio Grande Valley, Texas

I'm sitting in my backyard at 7 am on a Saturday, watching
thick morning fog that clearly ate too many double-wide
marshmallows the night before. Expanding to occupy more space

more than I imagine I ever could, even in an empty place like this.
In a vegetable field post-harvest season, I pick at my polka-dot hoodie,
unraveling the navy blue thread from the spot where my Tía Tina stitched

a hole shut. She was always so good at bringing our family together
at dinner time, back when I still ate regularly. I watch the neighborhood
behind me act like a thief who got away. This fog resembles leftover milk

in a cereal bowl. Perhaps, this fog is the glare in my eyes from the night
I couldn't find my way home, intoxicated by too many shots of flirtatious banter
poured by a politician who spun words like a carousel. I'm spinning and spilling

out all that is in me. Evaporating like dew, clinging to a sense of grounding.
Defying gravity. Finding myself suspended between Earth and sky, between
this place and that, always conscious of the space I take up and how the

                    space doesn't even know I'm here.

White Handed

kids
with
white skin
and
brown blood
don't
get
caught
red-handed
nobody's
keeping
an eye on them
in
the
corner
store
they
get away
with
crimes
their
primos
can't

As Seen on TV

My reflection on the television screen seized a strand of my
hair. Slidding it between freshly licked pursed lips. Pushing it
through the eye of a needle. Stitching me to a canvas white as
silence, pale as envy. Told me to sit still until they were done.
Told me it would hurt less if I just sit. There is a word for
this, I'm sure. When others make something else out of your
still-growing parts. The parts of you that will never stop grow-
ing, if you're lucky. They weave with my hair a tongue thin as a
kite string. Anchoring down brown versions of the American
Dream. Adding weight to conjugations and pageantry and
factual accounts of history. A kite string, so delicate, it blends
in the border between what was me and what was only my re-
flection, as seen on TV. All the while, they reminded me that
the pain would hurt less if I'd just sit still.

Awkward Date #1

"I mean, you *look* like you're from the valley," my date's best friend tells me
as we're seated for dinner.

By this statement, I imagine he means

        my drapes don't match my speech

I have reassure myself that what he means

        my eyes see straight through his bullshit

            He never bothers to explain himself.

//Fever Dream 2020//

Hard talks with hard hearts// Deciding who gets what months after the breakup// Forgetting roadmaps on palms I used to trace// Spending hours alone after dark on the River Walk// Smoking too much// Snowfall where it never snows// Potty training the new puppy who cries when left alone// Friends visiting from out of state// We shouldn't travel anymore// The news becomes concerning// Regularly scheduled programming// Interrupted// Buy a desk to work from home// Last supper in public at a brunch spot// Businesses close// Schools close// Masks don't work// Empty streets// Empty hair dye boxes// Purple shampoo// I haven't left home in weeks// Work is piling up// Tens of thousands dead// Countless more dying// Masks maybe work// Filing fingernails with teeth// Picking scabs with what could have been// Fidgeting legs from indecision// My hands won't stop shaking// Too aware of the Earth's quick spinning// Fall asleep gripping the mattress// Headaches// Vomiting// My prescription doesn't work// Crying doesn't work// Masks do work// Panic attacks alone on the River Walk// Civilians are being killed by cops// Judge and jury is being denied// Judge and jury deny justice// Protests// Fires// Helicopters circle downtown like vultures outside my window// Everything is exposed down to the bare bones// Floods of people pool between skyscrapers// A storm so terrible the power goes out// Ghosts in the hallway asking for directions// We are all lost// I cover my ears// I close my eyes// I open my mouth and sing// And cry// And manage to survive until morning// Then// The sun comes out again// Muddy puddles at my feet// Leftover rain on the roof dripping off the roof ledge// Condensation lingering on the windows// Smell of wet grass// Mockingbirds sing to teach me lessons// By early May, it already feels like mid-summer of next year//

My Accent (or lack thereof)

My accent is a chameleon, changing
to match the color of its surroundings,

sounding rushed and vibrant among
brown. Starched and crisp amid white.

A prism of speech is on my tongue,
ranging from the puro-pinche-party vowels

to my pinky-fingers-out-at-tea-time
enunciations of names like

Tía Lydia becomes
Tee-yuh Ee-yuh leaves my mouth

My tongue is a pendulum, swaying from side to side,
conforming to how I am expected to sound.

Laurel, my father's name.
Laurel, the name I offer to coffee shop baristas.

Growing up, we were told what brown people could eat in a white
people's world was the only way to get a seat at the dinner table.

Now I wish I was starving. I don't
even remember how I sound.

My natural voice is a phantom, a shadow.
My mouth is a stage for masked performers

putting on a production. They perform so well, but
who they are behind the façade. Who am I behind

my ever-shifting speech, an act of survival. I don't know,
except to say I sound like whoever I'm around.

I Have Lost My Way

I.
I carved my footsteps out of marble stone
paved the way for a past I won't run back to, yet
somehow stumble back when intoxication
in my peripheral view tugs me in its direction

Those strides were hard, taken by generations
who came before, ascending the moutain
from the valley below, singing songs of
deliverance made to get me this far

A people once slaves set free
to the dawn where sorrows were offered up
Night giving up her ways and sunlight
made visible the crooked way leading to
better days

I have lost my way

II.
I carved my heartbeat from glass,
sinking it deep into a riverbed
washing away the ways it remembered to
always be grateful

Flawed to count my blessings, I don't thank
and greet sickness and health
I draw water from orange dirt, leading cattle to
higher ground in the rain, shooting a rifle, skining the deer,
tending my wounds to heal while toiling harder

I have lost my way

III.
I carved my suffix onto porcelain veneer
As a third generation I ate my fill, squandered
the land, planting out of season, letting fields
wither away

I've paid no mind to the changing seasons
paid the cost to have chores done for me
turned my back to the path bridging the place where

I came from, a place where I'd forgotten my ways. My name feasted
until nothing was left in the storehouses then starved
and felt my bones protrude like mountains over valleys

A valley

I have fallen back into

selling myself short compared

to what my

'buelos suffered to carry

this name

I have lost my way

El Tercero

i am a napkin doodle
based on a watercolor
portrait inspired by
an oil painting
masterpiece that
never thought itself

bound to canvas

Gumíto

On days like these
I wish I was around people
who called me *Gumíto*

People around me—on days like these,
in places like these—
can't always pronounce the short version of my first name correctly
so I know it's too much to ask of them
to call me *Gumíto*

Gumíto isn't in their vocabulary,
and I'm too old to want to be called by this name but they don't need to know that

I long for someone here
to call me *Gumíto*

Hearing someone call me this way
       makes me think of how my great-grandparents survived the Mexican lynchings
       makes me think of how my grandparents toiled in fields to put food on tables not their own
       makes me think of how my parents worked long hours to give me a good education

Yet, here I am–
a struggling artist in a city where smooth hands and tongues get tangled like nooses
when trying to say only the first half of my full name

I wish someone here
could call me *Gumíto*

My grandfather heard his name "Gumíto!"
before he served a country willing to place its soldiers on the frontlines because of their brown skin

My father heard his name "Gumíto!"
before he worked tirelessly in an AC shop to bring home a paycheck to his mother and sister

I heard my name "Gumíto!"
before I was told to leave the swimming pool while the white kids were allowed to stay

Gumíto is an innocent name that knows how to bleed
picks up the pieces
starts over again
works hard
loves gently
calls out bullshit
judges with mercy
breaks everything apart when it's put together incorrectly

I wish someone here
knew my name

A Poem Written in San Antonio, Texas

The fray of my polka-dot hoodie makes perfect company on walks
beneath teaspoons of sugar, moonlight far
from sweet, somewhere between South Alamo Street and Saint Mary
I light a candle, pray the panic attack does not glide in while sailing
over concrete beside the River Walk

Perhaps tonight will be better than last night

We've hit the time of year when there's a lot more night than day
This presents opportunities for better nights *(or not)*

The echoes over the river surface, swirl and widen, and though I can't see the ducks
I hear their presence. I know they're there, and I wonder if people perceive me
the same when I disappear, when all they hear
from me are memes, double-taps, and Tiktoks—
the only trace of still-alive anyone can find of me

It's not that I don't want to be seen, it's just that
I don't want to be found.

Heart of Rose Gold

I have a heart of rose gold
A boy like me is not a dime a dozen
I'm told that floral arrangements are prayers
to those in hospitals, to those who've managed another year
So, I keep this vase brimming with holy water
mixed with tears from saints with thorn-pricked thumbs

Years spent away from home stay fresh in my mind–
alleys behind bars, faces I will never have names for

A stranger once told me that I am on a different frequency
Perhaps that's why no one ever seems to tune in when I speak
I light a candle, hoping someone turns the dial on their radio
so they can jam with me

But then I remember, it's flowers that do the trick. . . .
I walk the meadow, a forest long ago, reminding myself
how every empty place used to be full

I prove this theory with a two-sided coin when I fill my palm with
little pink flowers, the kind that grow wild in Texas, which I tame
with a pinch and a pluck and wrangle them with a lasso-bow to
magic-trick them into a bouquet

I lay them in the place where I first learned to tie my shoes
in the same cemetery where, when I visit home,
I leave flowers for strangers who were not always so

My rose gold heart, *my prayer*

One I hope someone is tuning in to hear
while in this vase, I offer another tear.

For Natalie

I
Orange marigolds were one of your favorites so I illuminate
your tombstone into a sunset and talk
to you for another hour while there's still light out
Our conversation is interrupted by an elderly woman who tells me
truest friends still surround us after we've died, and
I wonder how different it would be if everything hadn't turned out this way

I send you a message after years of voiceless absence—
the truck ride home

Years before, this patch of grass was freshly turned soil
melting into mud when many of us stood here in the rain
with flower petals in our hands, bidding you
farewell as you were lowered, mariachi playing
a sobbing accompaniment

Your little sister asked why, and no one had the answer
not even a silent god at Mass that morning

Days before, we were the silent ones, sitting multiple nights
at the viewing of your oil paintings,
memorial floral arrangements filled the stage
like a dense brush. I tucked a stuffed penguin beside you
when it was my turn for final goodbyes

Your body lay there without a word

The night before, amid roaring laughter, we remembered you
—people who had not seen each other for years, as if time
had not separated us—

Once family who became strangers
Once family again for this reunion

II
Shock
is what struck me first when
I scrolled through my contacts to tell everyone the news
Each person confused over why I was calling
and then fell silent
when I shared my reason—

> *A truck ride home before sunrise*
> *A drunk driver at the wheel*

The morning news report made me throw up
when it revealed the ambulance you were wheeled into
I didn't know who to call first, whether I was supposed
to call someone or cry or go back to bed, or
find something breakable to smash against the wall

There are pieces to us I will never get back

After so many years of silence, you suddenly reappeared
the night before you died—
your smile like I always knew it, a sunrise
on my Facebook of "people you may know"

It had been years since the fork in the road when
we went our separate ways. It was my fault
for the distance

I wanted to message you to inquire
about your life

But I didn't
I stayed quiet

Now, I can't stop apologizing to you for my silence.

Awkward Date #2

He calls me exotic like

    I'm the fucking parrot to his pigeon

    Spanish teacher in his favorite daddy issues Twitter account

I want to wreak havoc on his windshield and teach him a lesson.

Millennial Approaching Mid-Life

Polvorones con chochitos haven't tasted good
since I was a kid. Candy sprinkle constellation

sanctuaries. Purple mountains beneath cafecito eyes,
they've never drooped this low before. Plum circles

royal rings, designer bags. This is what old skin
feels like when you lose the color you are born

with. Because there's more night than day and you
spend all day inside, in front of a rectangular screen

glowing like a snowstorm supernova. You have no
life anymore. This is what old skin feels like when

it's worn by thirty-something-year-old bones. Hard
as telling the truth. Easier said than done. I never take

my own advice. So, everyone else's grass will always
be greener than mine. I live my life in the clouds. Stoned

air sign. Scales with some chill, I guess. Because mercy
triumphs over judgment. At least that's what I tell

myself when all the world feels like a courthouse,
and I think I could use some order in my life.

Standardized Testing

I fill in the box labeled Hispanic darker than I do the box labeled *White*.

Standardized testing shouldn't require a guilt trip.

Untitled

My parents kept a secret from their children,
sour copper in their mouths from biting their tongues.
When we grew up frustrated by the penalties for living
Chicanx in America, we didn't have a word for it.

My mother hid her tears beneath the mattress.
I found them when my dying grandmother
spoke only Spanish and my tongue
could not produce a clear "por siempre."

My father boxed away his shouts in the attic.
I found them when I grew tired of pretending I didn't hear
outsiders talking shit aimed at people from the borderlands.
There is a word for every emotion, its own language.

Every feeling is a brick, and we build fortresses in certain seasons.
I am my own captive for months on end when I can't cry
or yell my way out of everything I am feeling.
There is a word for this, I'm sure.

Self-Destructive Tendencies

tender kneecaps & ashy elbows. scraped burgundy, crimson and gritty asphalt. stardust spilling out of me. rolling. vulnerable. high-risk. precarious as ever. poorly handled. precious cargo. drop me from up high. pull me back down low. push my way to the front of the line. this is mine. this is my time. and i am lost. soon to be found. prolonged process. thinning patience. dumpster dive. washroom spun crazy. dirty sheets. clean conscience. body soap and shampoo and conditioner. three-in-one. zero tea. little shade. tough meat. made tender. beat up. black & blue. i repeat the process. a chance to earn myself a heart of gold.

A Poem Written in Corpus Christi, Texas

steady hum
melody
rings me dreams
without lyrics
shore at high tide
makes me wonder
what you see
when i watch
you sleep
sand-dune cheeks
sandcastle smile
an ocean rests
between us,
but ocean wakes
are how
lonely islands
learned their sense
of touch
within reach
out of sight
distance
our favorite illusion
& i wonder
how you'll leave me
how this
will eventually
come to an end
scent of eucalyptus
lilac stargazers
angel breaths
filling my bedroom
i know
vase water
will run dry
one day
nothing left
but worn-bone

calcium rings
measuring how
short our time
together grows
haunting countdown
circles moving
lower and lower
i know
this is
me
maybe just
how i am
always will be
wondering
why
i prefer sunset
to sunrise

Bus Station

Humble last bets. If this meant anything to you,
you'd put up a fight. Would not be conservative

with the volume of your voice or hold back when
you should rush forward. I waited outside the bus

station for you. As if you might arrive. Pretending
you would. I should know better by now. Always

taking the longest route home to enjoy one last puff
before bed. Ashing out our alternate reality. Where

you didn't confuse good green for the greener side
of imaginary white picket fences. You never cared

for boundaries anyway. And away I went with
the sleeping, once-jubilant butterfly in my gut. In my

head, I vomited the promises I would have kept
if you had shown up. Then swallow them whole.

I drove away out of the bus station parking lot,
finding myself merely along for the ride.

Summer 2015

Major Lazer & DJ Snake &
when "Lean On" burns the air,
melt like spilled raspa
between cracks, fill
in gaps / in alibi
emotional distance
space between Pluto and god
dance floors are studio flats
pliers are shower knobs
homemade pesto on paper plates
neon lighters & dust bunnies
red wine & moving boxes
candles & countdowns

Leaning on the counter to say,
"It's getting late"
Leaning on your invitation
one last time

Following day
driving home
down I-35
red eyes, but
not high
Sitting on a mattress
on the floor
until midnight
needing to unpack
an apartment
I don't belong to
Trying to fit in
between inhale and heartbeat

Leaning on the exhale to say,
"It's getting late"
Leaning on your absence
for the first time.

Drunk Texts

How is it that you still count with
your fingers to make sure siete is
seven and mumble through the
Spanish parts of every Shakira song

    Shot glass, needle

    Don Julio, thread

Sew tonight a memory, one
you'll lose before sky burns to blue

    La luna, she will remember you this way

    El sol, he's always late to the party

A bouquet of drunk texts to no one and
everyone. Petals strung across the floor.

Bedtime Prayer

it feels like the universe isn't showing up for me i send out the good my body holds
in every direction i see lacking love like rain i water the thorn bush and dandelion
both nurture what can't nurture me back lay down my crown for the pauper tell
the rustle in my trees goodnight do not tell the wind which way she should go let
the night play out the way she chooses to flow never try to control the stars and
their placement and though maybe it's selfish i do still whisper my wishes to them
politely never speaking out of turn always quick to listen first taming my tongue
has played a vital role in telling the universe how much i love it even when i feel
like it doesn't love me back even if this life is a toxic relationship i'm too scared to
cut off even when none of my wishes come true asking to break a twenty dollar
bill handed back a couple bucks and some pocket lint yet outside my window
a whisper returns back to me from the rustle in my trees before falling asleep

i love you, goodnight.

A Poem Written in South Padre Island, Texas

I

best

remember

breaths synced

with crashing waves in

a dome tent after midnight. Camping

on an island in the Gulf of Mexico. Our back and

forth. Inhales and exhales. Entwined with what the tide offered

and reclaimed. My push, your pull. Dependent on the moon humming over us.

Her pearl necklace glowed with countless scattered pieces mirrored on the gulf surface.

Unceasing waves reflecting our back and forth. And the universe had never

before felt quite so small and quite so big. Our placement in it. Two

satellites dancing for a brief moment. Our own gravity to one

another. Lifting me up just to drop me back down

because at the end of the day that is our

pull on each other ever was. We blamed

the G and molly for those midnights

on the island, but it was

only ever the cosmos

alive in

us

Depression on Repeat

i ate one slice of 7-11 pizza for
breakfast, lunch and dinner
yesterday / today / again

my aching desert too full of empty space
accent hidden in cave of wonders back of throat
suspicious of people who can sleep all night long
       abandoned building broken window smile
       colbalt & windshield & wiper & rainfall
       kite gliding by thrift store clothing racks
       longing to belong

rose glitter sequin in clammy earthquake hands
always looking for the nearest emergency exit
everything you'd expect a queer chicano to be
       in a country that he was born in
       in a country that tells him to go back
       to where he came from as if such a place
       ever existed

i want to go home
yesterday / today / again

Mentiroso

You can't spell *mentiroso*

without *men*

A Poem Written in Middle of Nowhere, Texas

Rocker couple adorned in oil-stained bandanas
and smudged flame tattoos are liberal with kisses
outside of the area where the men's and women's
restroom entrance meet in a gas station in
Middle of Nowhere, Texas

One is quick to think, *how trashy!*

But, hear me out—

Imagine being so focused on holding someone's hands that the smell of urinal pucks
unable to mask the smell of Five Hour Energy urine doesn't make you want
to vomit. Even the tile grime germs aren't enough to dissuade you
from rubbing your lips like it's five o'clock somewhere
in the same vicinity as bleach and un-flushed shit

I believe there is a time and a place for everything, but—

Imagine being so lost in someone else's voice that your brain's chemicals
break down the sensible universe walls of the box we sit in, making you
forget about the past and future. At present, nothing about
cesspool gas station bathrooms matters. The only law of
science you abide by is gifting the other person
affection, regardless of what it looks
like on the outside

I know this all sounds crazy, but—

Imagine being in love.

Culture Vulture

Culture vulture social media influencers, your white magic is your privilege. It is a power you don't have to lift a finger to stir. Gentrifies stealing traditions from your brown neighbors like their recipes are clothes left hanging out to dry. Wearing them proudly online for everyone to like share and subscribe. Parading their knowledge as your own. Using their history to advance your own financial endeavors.

Wobbly-Footed Huapangos through the Dollar Tree

I.
Shuffling through an aisle of probably stale potato chips
from a brand no one has ever heard of, I check
one item off my list. I am sad I will have no one
to hold my hair back when I inevitably throw them up.
Yet, I blame my indecisive self when I consider it's because I swipe left on
anyone who swipes right on me. Anyone I swipe
right on will eventually have me left on read.

I pick out another nail polish to add to my collection—
glittery red.
It makes me think of ruby slippers
& unexpected trips
& how my mid-thirties is a tornado I wasn't prepared for
& how maroon fits me better, but

it's unnecessary to match my exterior to my expectations when
so much is out of alignment.

This will be the only public place I will go to until next week when I need actual groceries.

I pick out a fishbowl for something I'll eventually DIY—I don't know what yet
& AAA batteries for the television remote
& envelopes for letters I'll never get around to buying stamps for
& blue dish soap
& green gel pens
& a happy birthday balloon just because.

The list doesn't matter at this point.
I've learned that what I set out for won't be what I get anyway—

> *I have the kind of sadness that is amplified when things start to go right.*

When things I want start wanting me back, I collect them like lightning bugs
in a mason jar to light my night as long as I keep them close to me.

I am most guarded when I have more to lose.

Because nobody's excitement matches mine when I share projects
I've worked hard to complete.
Because you're more likely to be bitten by a mosquito
when kissing in the rain.

II.
I water my dying peace lily for the second time this week.
She's been wilting for months, but here we are—
she's thirsty, always on her last breath, and I get it.

I, too, know the flavor of a last meal,
a caramelized layer of fish sauce coating tofu, the
back of throat post vomit brandy sting after deciding
today isn't the day.

I remember playing in trees growing up, with outstretched arms
and hands gripping thick branches meant
there was still a chance for a better view.
Now I spend days sitting at the base of trees building cairns, waiting for something—

I don't know what yet.

living a perpetual sunset
always on the verge of
whatever comes next.
lingering tangerine
streaks holding up violet.
sky. weightless. chill
wind that is in no rush to get
to where it's going.
and i think leaves stay
green in texas for longer
than they should. red light
pause before yielding to
yellow. hesitant as smoke
rings in the backseat.
wavering booming stereo
from the dashboard. my
hand out the passenger
side window. gliding on
the hope that tonight will
be better than last night.
believing it could be,
because you promised.

A Conversation With Myself

Maybe we're in two different places. Along for the ride. A long way to drive. Fork in the road. Knife the divide. Maybe. Just maybe.

Maybe we're too different to work. Two paradises of whispers and dirt. Lonely islands. Sinking ships. Drowning in seas we were told we could walk on. Maybe. Just maybe.

And maybe this is the start of something new. Isn't that how old habits die off, anyway? Bury me shallow. I'm sinking deep. Second guesses. Hours too long. Maybe what hurts like hell is the cost of a dream. Maybe. Just maybe.

Never (fill in the blank) Enough

When I write a poem
I always worry that it isn't

      brown enough
      queer enough
      chemical imbalanced Jenga block tower enough

      loud enough to advance the cause

When I write a poem
my identity becomes a tightrope

but I am a stringless kite

a
life
barreling
into cobalt cloud
cathedral subtle dew drop fortress
out of chest rapid twirl trailing
tail nosedive into mesquite
unpredictability's branches
enveloping jailhouse
miscalculated
assumption
held hostage
watching
sunset

A Poem Written in Austin, Texas

You wore sunglasses when we first met
Unintentionally making me wait until after sunset
To memorize
Your eyes
Walnut, ivory, twinkle of curiosity
Told me the things I wanted to hear with one glance

Blink once for yes, blink twice for maybe, no was not an option

Shoulder to shoulder
Your head resting on my shoulder
Secret knock asking to enter
Outside the bar, waiting to join max occupancy inside
Photographs of velvet green and red vintage furniture
Wine in rooms warmed by barrels of side glances
Until the night grew late
Settling into bed like dust settling over centuries of nights
Spent like this in make-believe spaces where
Distance is an illusion

Chest to chest
Your head nestled on my neck
We'll always have midnights & 2 am to 4 am
A spare room transformed ocean blue as the sun rose again
I could see a future in your shallow breaths
A deep current pulling me to where my feet couldn't touch the floor
Kicking for my life

Outside in the lane for departures
I prayed for seconds to stretch a little longer
When we both hesitated for a goodbye kiss that never came
I told myself this wasn't goodbye
It was only a moment that cascaded into

longing

Corazón Condominium

There are many stories in my heart
Each person I have met gets a place to live inside of me
Each resident is assigned to a specific unit

    #285 the stranger who gave me flowers
    because somewhere in the cosmos aliens make wishes upon our sun

    #427 the Lyft driver I gave directions to
    because it was her first week living in Austin, TX

    #936 the turtle who watched the sunset with me
    on the edge of Town Lake during the week I cried over butterflies in car grills

There are so many levels to my love
Each inhabitant who lives inside of me has toured my ups and downs
Each floor is designed for a specific intimacy

    #54 the level where I keep a glass bowl filled
    with rocks gifted to me by people I love and might never see again

    #12 the level for "this made me think of you"
    text messages and memes

    #95 3/4 the level where we have danced together
    in the shower and shared a single bath towel to dry off with

Corazón condominium
There are so many spaces for everyone to live in my heart

Maybe. Just Maybe

Sometimes, hanging in there means applauding everyone else's accomplishments. Community can have a way of making individuals feel extra excluded when not being offered a seat at the table. Going on YouTube to learn how to use a chainsaw to build yourself a place to eat. Going to bed hungry is not the least fair misfortune I have experienced because I have not always had a bed to sleep in. And for good measure, I believe the wind has a plan for all of us. It knows where it sweeps us off, so I make myself a dandelion and welcome the brokenness. Welcome the anxiety that comes with being shattered and spread thin as air. Ready to be let down again to figure out my own way to grow. Lift myself back up. Even if there are no ladder rungs to pull me up. With clenched fists and an open heart, I soar above the clouds, where the sun has no choice except to shine on me. Exposing my heart for all to see. I have stood in line waiting so long that my shoes have had a love affair with the ground. The only instances when the two parts are when I have to move aside for someone jumping the line. How often do I not get opportunities to move forward after trying my best and having nothing left to give.

Always saying yes
Always hearing no
Living for the word

Maybe. Just maybe.

One of the Old Names

Orange jello
turquoise masks
counting breaths to
ground myself
Paper bags
intestine tightrope
walking over stomach acid
Fluorescent stars
squeaky sneaker hallways
not your favorite place to be,
                but here you are
Plastic bracelets with your private information are
                      all the rave this autumn season
Here in the hospital, you lose your identity
                        become a number

But the lady at check-in asks me for my name

I tell her,
Gumecindo

She tells me,
You have one of the old names
They don't give those out anymore

It made me finally feel a part of something—
grounded   stable   rooted
homemade: DIY born
like I finally had a homeland at some point in the narrative
during the prequel
Like it's okay that this is how I'm spending my 35th birthday
I am the youngest person in the waiting room, but
I am used to this
blurry red eyes
tears blind me
earthquake hands
Nonetheless, stable-hearted

Assimilated Natives

I.
Assimilated Natives:

We do not speak with the sun-fire forbidden tongue of our fathers
as if we were not carved by broken promises and soothing songs within
            the nightfall womb of our mothers.

We were taught to sound like foreigners,
our whitewashed words paint a picture of a heritage
shattered into pieces
is as much as we can speak with our elders.

Blistered trails behind us are now burnt-out lantern smoke streams
first paved with stone and grit by those who came before us.
With each passing generation, our customs fade
and we are uncertain of where we came from.

II.
Assimilated Natives:

We are strangers to the land's true nature, unlike our 'buelitas,
who witness tall palms kissing clouds did not sprout in measured rows
Instinctively knowing divisions in fields led to what future generations would call
gentrification.

Worthless dirt wedged beneath worn brown fingernails suddenly became
costly when clinging to the polished brown boots of white men.

Citrus, an acidic plague, once used to lure tourists like stomach bug flies,
swarms swelling across international bridges demand that they be closed.

Nature, herself, pillaged by northern settlers
built over her iron-gated communities on the west side,
upwind from the natives
like *us*

Our kind is a stench in the foreigners' nostrils.

III.
Assimilated Natives:

Our brown skin is an empty playground at first sight
of orange street lights flickering their eyes open.
We are unnaturally pale,
we should have much more depth to us.

We hide from the sun to prevent it from getting *too* dark,
scrubbing our skin with soap twice as hard so
we will have better opportunities as adults.

When it's time to succeed in school or get a job
the more you look like your teachers and employers, the better your chance!
*   And if you can sound like them, you'll surely pass for one of their own!*

Our tongues are divided in two and sewn back together,
stitched with phrasings and names
kay-pass-ah
chips and kay-so
laurel

We survive in a world blossoming like marigolds in summer radiance,
erupting from the grave of our traditions.
Just because you cannot read this land's writing
does not mean the gravestone is silent.

The land cries out what we already know—we have always been here
doing what they call new, what is labeled
as the latest trend.

Our broken backs in their flowerbeds,
the sweat of our brows, we share
this fate that befell our elders,
laboring in ache for the prosperity of white men.

IV.
Assimilated Natives:

We must relight our lanterns and
search for the trails behind us,
retrace the beats of our hearts until they
tell the stories of who we are, where we come from—
the might of our lineage,
the fight of our call.

Let it echo down the river to the Gulf
that we are here, that we remember we vowed
to find our way home
and refuse to assimilate any further.

Latinx Twitter Feud

I witness a cis, straight, white-passing Chicano
scold a Chicana college student as if she's a
misbehaved kindergartner for pronouncing

> *Latin-ex instead of Latin-equis*

& it's like
this is precisely why a simple letter can serve as a sword
and shield because I don't believe he'd have been so
condescending toward the college student were she a
cis Chican-o and not a Chican-a

& it's like
having cis white skin that colors inside the lines makes
you think you're always right because you were never told "no"
growing up

& it's like
you've never had to speak clear English absent of a valley
accent to get through checkpoints without being asked to
pop open your trunk because you've never sounded like the
ones their ears are to the ground for

& it's like
you don't know how it is to live in a divide
where a single letter can give you a fighting
chance

Nobody cared to inform the cis, straight, white-passing Chicano
that there is more than one way to pronounce a word
that holds a multitude of identities. It's everyday life for some of us.

Awkward Date #3

"No, but, like, where are you *originally* from?"
He asks a typical first-date question.

"I'm originally from the valley."
I tell him as he sips his whiskey soda.

"Really?"
He could sound no more surprised than if I had used brujeria
to tell him the last four digits of his social.
He's the sort of guy you know *for sure* has a social.

"But you don't sound like you're from the valley."
He explained his shock as if
I should be obliged by what he considered a compliment.

I sip my vodka sprite
Squiggly-line grin and continue
to other boring topics, but
not before ordering my final drink, an
adios, motherfucker.

Ode to a Toxijoto

I drink pendejo juice on the regular
Pero, like, you know what? Maybe that's just my favorite
taste for day-to-day
living la vida sonsa.
Watch me tell that man I like him for real after our first date.
What's his last name again?
Is he the one with the Silverado?
or the one who's always getting high on his own supply?

I don't know, sis. Pero this pendejo juice tastes like the night is barely getting started.

Watch me post a fire selfie to Snapchat–kissy lips, booty perky,
and use the filter that makes my skin glow like leche quemada–
he'll eat this shit up like a lollipop.
My subtle Midnight Magic bat signal in the clouds
and I light a candle and pray he sees it
porque I want him to know
what's up and that I'm still up.

Oh, he viewed my selfie and didn't jump into my DM's?!
How fucking rude is this pinche vato?!
Watch me take otro shot of pendejo juice when I start to DM
all these other thirsty men who've been hitting me up since 10 pm

Aye, pero hold up, my man, my PP956ALVC valluco valiente,
he right now double-tapped my most recent selfie on Instagram,
dropping me a hint, so I double-tap his most recent pic, too.
Puro pinche pachanga in my pansa while waiting for a response.
Borracho butterflies in me do huapangos when he DM's me on Snap:
You up?

Yes, I'll be right over, papi
It's 2 am and I'm already in bed
I work at 8 am
Pero, like, you know what?
This pendejo juice tastes like bad decisions, and it's bottoms up for me.

Osea, I Speak Border

A man I don't even know from L.A. who studied language
corrects my Spanish, and I do not bother to explain that this is how
                        actual Chicanxs from the border actually speak

I feel the way golden eagles did when they saw the first airplane.

I feel the way peaceful snakes did when they learned they symbolized the devil.

I feel the way prickly pear cacti do when domesticated into clay pots
                                 for decoration on high-rise patios.

I feel like the moon that's been walked all over.

                   My tongue isn't a street corner for you to gentrify.

Non-Academic Artists

When asked about their favorite artist, non-academic artists may mention someone
that academic artists may not know, or deemed cliché. This is because academic artists
are taught to praise one of equal stature or greater merit even if they are not known.

Non-academic artists teach themselves at their own pace. They learn from used books,
word of mouth and blog sites, and other writers. Unfortunately, some of these writers
see them as competition and talk negatively about them. But, non-academic artists are wise
in their own right, walk their unmarked trails, acknowledging those who came before them,
some who did not have college degrees either. Still, they are the subject of many essays
written by academic artists who might have never roused at 4 am by a ghost, ready
to hand-feed them words of an unwritten poem.

Non-academic artists use social media like an atlas, navigating through the cultivation
of their craft. Anzaldúa and couplets find homes in workshops via Zoom, nestled in hashtags
referenced by their colleagues.

Non-academic artists do not look down upon the academic artist, although the reverse
is not always true. If given a choice to be cut open by a well-versed theorist or a dropout
with hands-on experience, I'd entrust my life to the hands whose fingers bare traces of dirt.

History

When white men say what happened,
it's called history.

When anyone else says what happened,
it's called an elective.

A Poem Written in San Isidro, Texas

I wore a crown and called it dirt. Told you to walk all over me
if my pride became too much for my own good. Because even kings
return to the earth that birthed them from soot and roots.

Lay me, oh, lay me in a bed of
laureles verdes y canciónes fuerte
to grow at my own pace, at my own time.

river veins / flowing / unfolding / like vines

until this land is claimed as mine
to echo ancestor's songs who sang before me.

Brujas on the Border

Sana, sana,
I'll make you heal, make you heal real good.
Bad is my intention, but
outcomes are what we judge by.
At the end of this spell,
I'll make you feel, make you feel real good.

You'll never see it coming. Never see me coming for you.
White egg shells rubbing
your sand dune body camouflaged
into my pale skin.

You'll never see me coming. Never see me coming for you.
When I swoop down from overhead, talons sharp
as judgmental eyes
and scoop you up. You are my
unsuspecting prey.
White feathers go invisible when morphing
back into my
pale skin.

Light a thousand candles, but you don't even have a prayer
You'll be on your knees worshipping and appeasing me
with flowers, partaking of my blood and body.
No matter how hard you whip your back
or fondle every bead within your desperate reach
your plea for mercy will fall on my deaf ears.

I promise, you don't even have a prayer.

River Prayer

My existence, this river flowing, expanding
and collapsing and drawing in, calling the sojourner,
the refugee, the one seeking a better life for their loved ones.
For who is not promised a hopeful tomorrow?

Within my skin, this river veins with bones
and determination and ideas striving to shine a light
into a world seeking to snuff out suns in the skies–
enduring flame burning even when waters rise.

This heart, my endless river, seamless
and sad and glad for it knows to hold tighter
than hands are willing to. It whispers and sings,
echoing laughter and tears, balancing, merging
sides. Uniting every link in the chain,
breaking every barrier that gets in its way.

Our valley, our river's lifeblood, heartbeat
and breath and movement. What summons the sun
to rise and moon to phase. Stars to guide the storm-
tossed home. Those lost. Those tired. Disconnected
from their roots. Struggling to thrive in lands not their own.

Like monarchs in flight seeking their destination,
call them home, river. Call them home.

      our essence—

        our river

our song—

        our river

           our source—

                our river

                    our life—

                      our river.

'Buela's Handiwork

'Buela's hands unaffected by flame
Mold the masa, flip and bake
Bless the forehead, push and shake
From womb to tomb remain, sustain.

Makeshift Cages

When
I was a
child
on the
border, we
tried
catching
green parrots
with
makeshift
cages

As an
adult,
men
in green
catch
children
on the
border and
put them in
makeshift
cages

My Heritage is La Llorona

We pass through the waters of the Río Grande,
She calls out her children. But we have deaf ears submerged

in lands on the other side of the border. She cries and
cries. No one replies that we are right here, mere

feet away yet worlds apart. Torn from her heart,
not knowing how to let go. Not knowing what to do except

mourn the loss, her own, our own. Imaginary lines drawn
in the sand. No one remains to cast the first stone.

Her blameless legacy gone. Children she hoped would carry
her name wander lost in the light. At night her wails await

our reply to say we are here. That we remember
her name, the sternness of her tenacity and recollection.

To tell her that we have not forgotten her sovereign tongue,
carving our hearts her name— *mi gente*

                                                         home.

A Poem Written in Marfa, Texas

driving six hours west// texas evolving// flat// hilly// mountainous the farther we get// cloudy dirt roads// periwinkle skies// choosing the safest hiking trail// unexpectedly clawing to the highest peak// howling like wolves off the ledge// howls stampeding across the rugged desert landscape// howls barreling back into our drummer boy chests// pah rum pah pum pum corazon// inspired by magic where magic had lost its voice// a solo yellow butterfly// yellow everything// yellow everywhere// bubble gum hair// champagne sunsets// red wine every night// splintered fingers// glitter green nail polish// cracking wood into pieces// crumpling pages torn from a journal// lighters on their last breath// campfires devouring the previous year behind us// walking into an open range and// asking where to next// fading teeth marks on my shoulder// branding into purple scars// erasing purple scars // letting go of what i shouldn't hold// watching kites fly// higher than the stars// i am the kite// but i am no longer stuck in the past// i make the nighttime sky skip ahead// a few beats// consider myself moving// forward// gliding// into the future// tethered to wind// with promise for tomorrow// wind taking me// from one place to the next // air that does not know how // to make me feel let down // air // i can finally breathe //again //

Forgiving Myself

I will forgive,
      breeze in my chest
      unintentional seed
      sprouting tornado

      springtime sunbeams
      accidental precursor
      to sunburn

To forgive myself,
      clear &
      cloudy &
      hurricane kissing stained glass window

Upon reflection,
      I see the words worth saying never
      caused the walls of anyone's home to crack.

Borderland Experiences are Not Universal

It's 9 pm on a Thursday night and I'm on Grindr
because I am young, gay, and out of town
and that's what you do when you're young, gay, and out of town
Except, I am not exactly visiting this place

I'm home
back in the borderlands

A cute boy messages me—*sup?*
I respond with an emoji. Yes. That emoji
Then, ask him what he's up to
He responds with—*waiting in line to get into Mexico*

And I think how it makes sense to me
because I'm not exactly visiting this place

I'm home
back in the borderlands

And in the borderlands, you wait in line at 9 pm on Thursdays to get into Mexico,
because that's where you go for cheap drinks
or medicine
or braces
or dinner,
and it makes no sense to anyone who has never called the borderlands home

Here at home,
we drink the pink medicine for stomachaches—and no, not Pepto—
the one in the clear bottle, ten-times stronger, your tía sneaks from across,
and we order a "botana for two,"
to feed a family of six

As a child, if you act up at HEB, your mom points
to the nearest, most disheveled stranger and tells you,
"They're gonna take you if you don't behave!"
Years later, when you bring it up to her, she'll tell you, "Ay, mentiroso."

You can drive through ten towns in twenty minutes,
and your 'buela, before you leave the house, prays for your safety
because this is considered a "road trip"

By thirty, your body instinctively wakes up early every Sunday to wait
in line for barbacoa, whether you crave it or not

We laugh louder than the chicharras in summer time,
sing more passionately than the grackles on the powerlines

We know, when you get a certain flutter in your chest,
hear the wind shift, it means it's time to listen
for danger. For whatever caused the songbirds
to hush. To wait and see if it's time to run and hide

When black helicopters circle the crop fields, and BP SUV's rush
like a stampede, and you, a the third generation with papers, it's still
in your blood to hide. Survive

We are a lively people, and the lively are best at surviving—
hurricanes, floods, fires, and outsiders with political agendas who think
they know what's best for us. They don't know about pink medicine, botanas,
or how our river moves when rain patterns change

How our river is like wind. A reverberating heart expanding,
collapsing with every inch she's caged by freestanding walls
that do nothing but divide

They don't know our land
They don't know our people

They don't know borderland experiences are not universal

My Skin

My skin is too light to be thought of as brown yet
too brown to fit in comfortably at dive bars on the gentrified eastside

My skin is generations of laborers suddenly repurposed
to fit the mold of what can be polished white

This light skin magnifies my blemishes and markings
makes you think I think I'm better, despite

every scar *showing*
every scrape *telling*

how I can't handle the sun burning me blood-red
when yours generously turns a couple tones bronzer—
dark around the sides, a glass mug containing a stout beer

This light skin makes me a glass house meant for throwing rocks at
broken to   p i e c e s   because I'm

not brown enough for the natives

not white enough for the foreigners

I am two halves   not whole

A split land divided   down the middle

One foot on   each side

Neither side makes me feel like I belong
I am not at home in my own skin

Discredited for

skin that doesn't know how to properly roll r's

Skin that draws racial slurs into its gravitational pull

Skin that tells you I am not brown enough

Skin that lies and says, "I am not brown at all."

Skin that makes me a treasure chest of secrets I can't bury deep enough to hide

You know where to find my truths
look no further because here I am

Two feet   in   two places

Slowly meeting   in the middle

On the   border of

here and there

Here, where *I come from*
there, where I am going
I am the merging
I am the coming together
at the center
of two lands *now* made one

My skin is a battleground where peace must be declared

Two warring sides
must make amends
so I can show off this skin, my wardrobe of two worlds
now one, where I am striving to be at home
and whole.

Little Joto

Little joto dancing on the border,
us queers never looked so razzle dazzle sugarplum fairy fly
swaying from one side to the other
to balance the tender and machismo so people won't give us too much
lip when they notice our arms are heroic you-won't-like-me-
when-I'm-angry shade of muscle green when it comes to giving hugs,
limp fideo when it comes to throwing a ball,
and kick it far.

Spackle sparkle twinkling as you dance on the border
of your two halves–neither is your true homeland.
Bake a cake with your tia's secret recipe of sweet sugar
and a velvet touch. Leave it in the oven until it chars into
big-boys-don't-cry tar. Spend time in a fragrant garden watered
by your tio's thumb kissing the manguera into a fountain,
stomp on the flowers on the way out, in and out,
crushed all over. You have been made to be the beat-down,
worn-out doormat by those who refuse to accept your jazzy sparkle,
who fail to grasp your folklorico flare, but they applaud
their toxic behavior disguised as I-know-what's-best-
this-is-for-your-own-good ignorance.

They have not seen you practice for hours, your bleeding toes
and broken bones. You persist practicing, keep on going–
the show must go on! Dance like all the chismosas are watching!

Pero you know what? You don't have a single care left to give
on the border of your two halves. You've inherited your mother's rose
petal lips, your father's summer-noon day eyes.

Send kisses to critics who raise their hands to push you down,
let them see your fiery gaze, they'll regret boxing you in,
convincing you to one plot or the other–

You belong in the divide, and the border
is your stage where you dazzle

onlookers who come for a show:
Give them a show!
The performance of your life!

This is your life—

a balancing act on the border of your two halves.

A Heritage Reborn

There is comfort when I feel wind on my back
while standing on the bridge that unites two places

In the moment of this in-between
I am not in one place or another
       I am in both

This place where sky and earth kiss like new lovers
                              where river and gulf embrace like old friends
    Here I am everywhere all at once

In perfect balance, exact symmetry
             far is close, wide is slim
     I come to the end of myself where I truly begin

I am not one way or another   I am possibilities combined

I am an undeniable past, a forgetful present, a promising future

I see the road behind me clearly and celebrate my origins
I see the road before me clearly and celebrate where I am headed

Once standing on the bones of forgotten ancestors, I now remember them
Once separating natural accent from foreign language, I now merge them
Once slouching, I stand tall

This is my legacy–a heritage reborn
from a generation refusing walls

We've replanted ourselves in fields where we've been uprooted,
stitched tears in the seams, stood our ground
with the double-edged sword in our mouths
recalled and retold what we've forgotten
remembered once more and vowed to

never forget.

Author's Biography

Gume is a Texan, native to the Río Grande Valley (Weslaco) on the southernmost border. For the past decade, he has dedicated himself to crafting literary works that promote inclusion and provoke further introspection into the complexities of culture and intersectional identities. The bulk of Gume's writings focuses on underrepresented groups, especially those representative of the communities he is a part of: Latinx and LGBT+. His published work includes both young adult fiction and poetry. Gume draws much of his inspiration from growing up on the border, and from the use of balancing multiple—and often conflicting—identities, to the use of rivers and Chicanx folklore. The Río Grande Valley's impact on Gume's writing is undeniably visible. In addition to writing, Gume regularly takes part in author visits in public schools and libraries, participates in literary panels, and does what he can to promote reading and writing. Currently, Gume lives in San Antonio, Texas, where he can be found either typing away on his laptop or getting lost on a hiking trail with his dogs Blu and Mouse.